Mediterranean Pasta and Rice Cookbook

Quick and easy Mediterranean diet recipes for your lunch with Pasta, Rice, Grain and Couscous to build healthy habits

Italian Cuisine

Table of Contents

Linguine with Artichokes and Peas

Rigatoni with Pancetta and Veggie

Orecchiette with Italian Sausage and Broccoli

Orzo with Shrimp and Feta Cheese

Toasted Barley and Almond Pilaf

Herbed Barley with Nuts

Brown Rice and Lentils

Brown Rice Pilaf

Wild Parmesan Mushroom Risotto

Basmati Rice with Currant and Almond

Basmati Rice with Pomegranate and Cilantro

Basmati Rice and Vermicelli Pasta Pilaf

Brown Rice with Red Pepper and Onion

Rice with Oranges, Green Olives, and Almonds

Rice Salad with Asparagus and Parsley

Polenta with Parmesan Cheese

Barley Pilaf with Parsley and Chives

Barley with Carrots, Snow Peas, and Sunflower Seeds

Barley Risotto with Parmesan cheese

Farro with Lemony Parsley and Mint

Warm Farro with Mushrooms and Shallot

Farro with Fennel and Parmesan Cheese

Farro with Asparagu, Snap Peas, and Tomato

Farro with English Cucumber, Yogurt, and Mint

Farrotto with Parmesan Cheese

Oregano Wheat Berries with Veggie

Wheat Berry Salad with Orange and Veggie

Wheat Berry Salad with Figs and Nuts

Mediterranean Lentils and Brown Rice

Wild Mushroom Farrotto with Parmesan

Barley Pilaf with Mushrooms

Moroccan-Style Brown Rice and Chickpea

Buckwheat Groats with Root Vegetables

Farro Risotto with Fresh Sage

Asparagus and Grape Tomato Pasta

Prep time: 10 minutes | Cook time: 25 minutes | Serves 6

8 ounces uncooked small pasta, like orecchiette (little ears) or farfalle (bow ties)

1½ pounds (680 g) fresh asparagus, ends trimmed and stalks chopped into 1-inch pieces

1½ cups grape tomatoes, halved

2 tablespoons extra-virgin olive oil

¼ teaspoon freshly ground black pepper

¼ teaspoon kosher or sea salt

2 cups fresh Mozzarella, drained and cut into bite-size pieces

1/3 cup torn fresh basil leaves

2 tablespoons balsamic vinegar

1. Preheat the oven to 400ºF (205ºC).

2. In a large stockpot, cook the pasta according to the package directions. Drain, reserving about ¼ cup of the pasta water.

3. While the pasta is cooking, in a large bowl, toss the asparagus, tomatoes, oil, pepper, and salt together. Spread the mixture onto a large, rimmed baking sheet and bake for 15 minutes, stirring twice as it cooks.

4. Remove the vegetables from the oven, and add the cooked pasta to the baking sheet. Mix with a few tablespoons of pasta water to help the sauce become smoother and the saucy vegetables stick to the pasta.

5. Gently mix in the Mozzarella and basil. Drizzle with the balsamic vinegar. Serve from the baking sheet or pour the pasta into a large bowl.

6. If you want to make this dish ahead of time or to serve it cold, follow the recipe up to step 4, then refrigerate the pasta and vegetables. When you are ready to serve, follow step 5 either with the cold pasta or with warm pasta that's been gently reheated in a pot on the stove.

Nutritional Facts Per Serving

Calories: 147g, Total Fat: 3g, Saturated Fat:1 g,Total Carbs: 17 g, Fiber: 5g, Protein: 16g, Sugar: 4g, Sodium : 420mg,Phosphorus: 337mg,Potassium: 290mg,Cholesterol: 8mg,

Triple-Green Pasta with Parmesan

Prep time: 10 minutes | Cook time: 14 minutes | Serves 4

8 ounces (227 g) uncooked penne

1 tablespoon extra-virgin olive oil

2 garlic cloves, minced

¼ teaspoon crushed red pepper

2 cups chopped fresh flat-leaf (Italian) parsley, including stems

5 cups loosely packed baby spinach)

¼ teaspoon ground nutmeg

¼ teaspoon freshly ground black pepper

¼ teaspoon kosher or sea salt

$1/3$ cup Castelvetrano olives, pitted and sliced

$1/3$ cup grated Pecorino Romano or Parmesan cheese

1. In a large stockpot, cook the pasta according to the package directions, but boil 1 minute less than instructed. Drain the pasta, and save ¼ cup of the cooking water.

2. While the pasta is cooking, in a large skillet over medium heat, heat the oil. Add the garlic and crushed red pepper, and cook for 30 seconds, stirring constantly. Add the parsley and cook for 1 minute, stirring constantly. Add the spinach, nutmeg, pepper, and salt, and cook for 3 minutes, stirring occasionally, until the spinach is wilted.

3. Add the pasta and the reserved ¼ cup pasta water to the skillet. Stir in the olives, and cook for about 2 minutes, until most of the pasta water has been absorbed. Remove from the heat, stir in the cheese, and serve.

Nutritional Facts Per Serving
Calories: 262g, Total Fat: 4g, Saturated Fat: 4g,Total Carbs: 51 g, Fiber: 13g, Protein: 15g, Sugar: 32g, Sodium: 1180mg,Phosphorus: 246mg,Potassium:1902 mg,Cholesterol: 3mg,

American Baked Ziti

Prep time: 15 minutes | Cook time: 43 minutes | Serves 8

For the Marinara Sauce:

2 tablespoons olive oil

¼ medium onion, diced

3 cloves garlic, chopped

1 (28-ounce / 794-g) can whole, peeled tomatoes, roughly chopped

Sprig of fresh thyme

½ bunch fresh basil

Sea salt and freshly ground pepper, to taste

For the Ziti:

1 pound (454 g) whole-wheat ziti

3½ cups marinara sauce

1 cup low-fat cottage cheese

1 cup grated, low-fat Mozzarella cheese, divided

¾ cup freshly grated, low-fat Parmesan cheese, divided

Make the Marinara Sauce

1. Heat the olive oil in a medium saucepan over medium-high heat.

2. Sauté the onion and garlic, stirring until lightly browned, about 3 minutes.

3. Add the tomatoes and the herb sprigs, and bring to a boil. Lower the heat and simmer, covered, for 10 minutes. Remove and discard the herb sprigs.

4. Stir in sea salt and season with freshly ground pepper to taste.

Make the Ziti

5. Preheat the oven to 375ºF (190ºC).

6. Prepare the pasta according to package directions. Drain pasta. Combine the pasta in a bowl with 2 cups marinara sauce, the cottage cheese, and half the Mozzarella and Parmesan cheeses.

7. Spread the mixture in a baking dish, and top with the remaining marinara sauce and cheese.

8. Bake for 30 to 40 minutes, or until bubbly and golden brown.

Whole-Wheat Couscous with Apricots

Prep time: 10 minutes | Cook time: 10 minutes | Serves 4

2 tablespoons olive oil

1 small onion, diced

1 cup whole-wheat couscous

2 cups water or broth

½ cup dried apricots, soaked in water overnight

½ cup slivered almonds or pistachios

½ teaspoon dried mint

½ teaspoon dried thyme

1. Heat the olive oil in a large skillet over medium-high heat. Add the onion and cook until translucent and soft.

2. Stir in the couscous and cook for 2 to 3 minutes.

3. Add the water or broth, cover, and cook for 8 to 10 minutes until the water is mostly absorbed.

4. Remove from the heat and let stand for a few minutes.

5. Fluff with a fork and fold in the apricots, nuts, mint, and thyme.

Penne with Tomato Sauce and Parmesan

Prep time: 10 minutes | Cook time: 50 minutes | Serves 6

1 shallot, sliced thin

¼ cup extra-virgin olive oil

2 pounds (907 g) cherry tomatoes, halved

3 large garlic cloves, sliced thin

1 tablespoon balsamic vinegar

1½ teaspoons sugar, or to taste

Salt and pepper

¼ teaspoon red pepper flakes

1 pound (454 g) penne

¼ cup coarsely chopped fresh basil

Grated Parmesan cheese

1. Adjust oven rack to middle position and heat oven to 350ºF (180ºC). Toss shallot with 1 teaspoon oil in bowl. In separate bowl, gently toss tomatoes with remaining oil, garlic, vinegar, sugar, ½ teaspoon salt, ¼ teaspoon pepper, and pepper flakes. Spread tomato mixture in even layer in rimmed baking sheet, scatter shallot over tomatoes, and roast until edges of shallot begin to brown and tomato skins are slightly shriveled, 35 to 40 minutes. (Do not stir tomatoes during roasting.) Let cool for 5 to 10 minutes.

2. Meanwhile, bring 4 quarts water to boil in large pot. Add pasta and 1 tablespoon salt and cook, stirring often, until al dente. Reserve ½ cup cooking water, then drain pasta and return it to pot. Using rubber spatula, scrape tomato mixture onto pasta. Add basil and toss to combine. Season with salt and pepper to taste and adjust consistency with reserved cooking water as needed. Serve with Parmesan.

Penne with Cherry Tomato and Arugula

Prep time: 15 minutes | Cook time: 50 minutes | Serves 6

1 shallot, sliced thin

¼ cup extra-virgin olive oil

2 pounds (907 g) cherry tomatoes, halved

3 large garlic cloves, sliced thin

1 tablespoon sherry or red wine vinegar

1½ teaspoons sugar, or to taste

Salt and pepper, to taste

¼ teaspoon red pepper flakes

1 pound (454 g) penne

4 ounces (113 g) baby arugula

4 ounces (113 g) Goat cheese, crumbled

1. Adjust oven rack to middle position and heat oven to 350ºF (180ºC). Toss shallot with 1 teaspoon oil in bowl. In separate bowl, gently toss tomatoes with remaining oil, garlic, vinegar, sugar, ½ teaspoon salt, ¼ teaspoon pepper, and pepper flakes. Spread tomato mixture in even layer in rimmed baking sheet, scatter shallot over tomatoes, and roast until edges of shallot begin to brown and tomato skins are slightly shriveled, 35 to 40 minutes. (Do not stir tomatoes during roasting.) Let cool for 5 to 10 minutes.

2. Meanwhile, bring 4 quarts water to boil in large pot. Add pasta and 1 tablespoon salt and cook, stirring often, until al dente. Reserve ½ cup cooking water, then drain pasta and return it to pot. Add arugula to pasta and toss until wilted. Using rubber spatula, scrape tomato mixture onto pasta and toss to combine. Season with salt and pepper to taste and adjust consistency with reserved cooking water as needed. Serve, passing Goat cheese separately.

Farfalle with Zucchini, Tomatoes, and Basil

Prep time: 10 minutes | Cook time: 20 minutes | Serves 6

2 pounds (907 g) zucchini and/or summer squash, halved lengthwise and sliced ½ inch thick

Kosher salt and pepper, to taste

5 tablespoons extra-virgin olive oil

3 garlic cloves, minced

½ teaspoon red pepper flakes

1 pound (454 g) farfalle

12 ounces (340 g) grape tomatoes, halved

½ cup chopped fresh basil

¼ cup pine nuts, toasted

2 tablespoons balsamic vinegar

Grated Parmesan cheese

1. Toss squash with 1 tablespoon salt and let drain in colander for 30 minutes. Pat squash dry with paper towels and carefully wipe away any residual salt.

2. Heat 1 tablespoon oil in 12-inch nonstick skillet over high heat until just smoking. Add half of squash and cook, stirring occasionally, until golden brown and slightly charred, 5 to 7 minutes, reducing heat if skillet begins to scorch; transfer to large plate. Repeat with 1 tablespoon oil and remaining squash; transfer to plate.

3. Heat 1 tablespoon oil in now-empty skillet over medium heat until shimmering. Add garlic and pepper flakes and cook until fragrant, about 30 seconds. Stir in squash and cook until heated through, about 30 seconds.

4. Meanwhile, bring 4 quarts water to boil in large pot. Add pasta and 1 tablespoon salt and cook, stirring often, until al dente. Reserve ½ cup cooking water, then drain pasta and return it to pot. Add squash mixture, tomatoes, basil, pine nuts, vinegar, and remaining 2 tablespoons oil and toss to combine. Season with salt and pepper to taste and adjust consistency with reserved cooking water as needed. Serve with Parmesan.

Spaghetti al Limone with Parmesan

Prep time: 10 minutes | Cook time: 15 minutes | Serves 6

½ cup extra-virgin olive oil

2 teaspoons grated lemon zest plus ⅓ cup lemon juice

1 small garlic clove, minced to paste

Salt and pepper, to taste

2 ounces (57 g) Parmesan cheese, grated

1 pound (454 g) spaghetti

6 tablespoons shredded fresh basil

1. Whisk oil, lemon zest and juice, garlic, ½ teaspoon salt, and ¼ teaspoon pepper together in small bowl, then stir in Parmesan until thick and creamy.

2. Meanwhile, bring 4 quarts water to boil in large pot. Add pasta and 1 tablespoon salt and cook, stirring often, until al dente. Reserve ½ cup cooking water, then drain pasta and return it to pot. Add oil mixture and basil and toss to combine. Season with salt and pepper to taste and adjust consistency with reserved cooking water as needed. Serve.

Spaghetti with Mussels and White Wine

Prep time: 10 minutes | Cook time: 25 minutes | Serves 6

1 pound (454 g) mussels, scrubbed and debearded

½ cup dry white wine

1 tablespoon extra-virgin olive oil

2 garlic cloves, minced

½ teaspoon red pepper flakes

1 teaspoon grated lemon zest plus 2 tablespoons juice

1 pound (454 g) spaghetti or linguine

Salt and pepper, to taste

2 tablespoons minced fresh parsley

1. Bring mussels and wine to boil in 12-inch straight-sided sauté pan, cover, and cook, shaking pan occasionally, until mussels open, about 5 minutes. As mussels open, remove them with slotted spoon

and transfer to bowl. Discard any mussels that refuse to open. (If desired, remove mussels from shells.) Drain steaming liquid through fine-mesh strainer lined with coffee filter into bowl, avoiding any gritty sediment that has settled on bottom of pan. Wipe skillet clean with paper towels.

2. Cook oil, garlic, and pepper flakes in now-empty pan over medium heat, stirring frequently, until garlic turns golden but not brown, about 3 minutes. Stir in reserved mussel steaming liquid and lemon zest and juice, bring to simmer, and cook until flavors meld, about 4 minutes. Stir in mussels, cover, and cook until heated through, about 2 minutes.

3. Meanwhile, bring 4 quarts water to boil in large pot. Add pasta and 1 tablespoon salt and cook, stirring often, until al dente. Reserve ½ cup cooking water, then drain pasta and return it to pot. Add sauce and parsley and toss to combine. Season with salt and pepper to taste and adjust consistency with reserved cooking water as needed. Serve.

Rigatoni with Thyme Beef Ragu

Prep time: 15 minutes | Cook time: 2½ hours | Serves 6

1½ pounds (680 g) bone-in English-style short ribs, trimmed

Salt and pepper, to taste

1 tablespoon extra-virgin olive oil

1 onion, chopped fine

3 garlic cloves, minced

1 teaspoon minced fresh thyme or ¼ teaspoon dried

½ teaspoon ground cinnamon

Pinch ground cloves

½ cup dry red wine

1 (28-ounce / 794-g) can whole peeled tomatoes, drained with juice reserved, chopped fine

1 pound (454 g) rigatoni

2 tablespoons minced fresh parsley

Grated Parmesan cheese

1. Pat ribs dry with paper towels and season with salt and pepper. Heat oil in 12-inch skillet over medium-high heat until just smoking. Brown ribs on all sides, 8 to 10 minutes; transfer to plate.

2. Pour off all but 1 teaspoon fat from skillet, add onion, and cook over medium heat until softened, about 5 minutes. Stir in garlic, thyme, cinnamon, and cloves and cook until fragrant, about 30 seconds. Stir in wine, scraping up any browned bits, and simmer until nearly evaporated, about 2 minutes.

3. Stir in tomatoes and reserved juice. Nestle ribs into sauce along with any accumulated juices and bring to simmer. Reduce heat to low, cover, and simmer gently, turning ribs occasionally, until meat is very tender and falling off bones, about 2 hours.

4. Transfer ribs to cutting board, let cool slightly, then shred meat into bite-size pieces using 2 forks; discard excess fat and bones. Using wide, shallow spoon, skim excess fat from surface of sauce. Stir shredded meat and any accumulated juices into sauce and bring to simmer over medium heat. Season with salt and pepper to taste.

5. Meanwhile, bring 4 quarts water to boil in large pot. Add pasta and 1 tablespoon salt and cook, stirring often, until al dente. Reserve ½ cup cooking water, then drain pasta and return it to pot. Add sauce and parsley and toss to combine. Season with salt and pepper to taste and adjust consistency with reserved cooking water as needed. Serve with Parmesan.

Warm Couscous

Prep time: 5 minutes | Cook time: 10 minutes | Serves 6

2 tablespoons extra-virgin olive oil

2 cups couscous

1 cup water

1 cup chicken or vegetable broth

Salt and pepper, to taste

1. Heat oil in medium saucepan over medium-high heat until shimmering. Add couscous and cook, stirring frequently, until grains are just beginning to brown, 3 to 5 minutes. Stir in water, broth, and 1 teaspoon salt. Cover, remove saucepan from heat, and let sit until couscous is tender, about 7 minutes. Gently fluff couscous with fork and season with pepper to taste. Serve.

Moroccan-Style Couscous with Peas

Prep time: 15 minutes | Cook time: 14 minutes | Serves 6

¼ cup extra-virgin olive oil, plus extra for serving

1½ cups couscous

2 carrots, peeled and chopped fine

1 onion, chopped fine

Salt and pepper

3 garlic cloves, minced

1 teaspoon ground coriander

1 teaspoon ground ginger

¼ teaspoon ground anise seed

1¾ cups chicken or vegetable broth

1 (15-ounce / 425-g) can chickpeas, rinsed

1½ cups frozen peas

½ cup chopped fresh parsley, cilantro, and/or mint

Lemon wedges

1. Heat 2 tablespoons oil in 12-inch skillet over medium-high heat until shimmering. Add couscous and cook, stirring frequently, until grains are just beginning to brown, 3 to 5 minutes. Transfer to bowl and wipe skillet clean with paper towels.

2. Heat remaining 2 tablespoons oil in now-empty skillet over medium heat until shimmering. Add carrots, onion, and 1 teaspoon salt and cook until softened and lightly browned, 5 to 7 minutes. Stir in garlic, coriander, ginger, and anise and cook until fragrant, about 30 seconds. Stir in broth and chickpeas and bring to simmer.

3. Stir in peas and couscous. Cover, remove skillet from heat, and let sit until couscous is tender, about 7 minutes. Add parsley to couscous and gently fluff with fork to combine. Season with salt and pepper to taste and drizzle with extra oil. Serve with lemon wedges.

Warm Pearl Couscous

Prep time: 5 minutes | Cook time: 17 minutes | Serves 6

2 cups pearl couscous

1 tablespoon extra-virgin olive oil

2½ cups water

½ teaspoon salt

1. Heat couscous and oil in medium saucepan over medium heat, stirring frequently, until about half of grains are golden brown, about 5 minutes. Stir in water and salt, increase heat to high, and bring to boil. Reduce heat to medium-low, cover, and simmer, stirring occasionally, until water is absorbed and couscous is tender, 9 to 12 minutes. Off heat, let couscous sit, covered, for 3 minutes. Serve.

Couscous with Lamb, Chickpeas, and Almond

Prep time: 20 minutes | Cook time: 24 minutes | Serves 6

3 tablespoons extra-virgin olive oil, plus extra for serving

1½ cups couscous

1 pound (454 g) lamb shoulder chops (blade or round bone), 1 to 1½ inches thick, trimmed and halved

Salt and pepper, to taste

1 onion, chopped fine

10 (2-inch) strips orange zest

1 teaspoon grated fresh ginger

1 teaspoon ground coriander

¼ teaspoon ground cinnamon

⅛ teaspoon cayenne pepper

½ cup dry white wine

2½ cups chicken broth

1 (15-ounce / 425-g) can chickpeas, rinsed

½ cup raisins

½ cup sliced almonds, toasted

1/3 cup minced fresh parsley

1. Adjust oven rack to lower-middle position and heat oven to 325ºF (163ºC). Heat 2 tablespoons oil in Dutch oven over medium-high heat until shimmering. Add couscous and cook, stirring frequently, until grains are just beginning to brown, 3 to 5 minutes. Transfer to bowl and wipe pot clean with paper towels.

2. Pat lamb dry with paper towels and season with salt and pepper. Heat remaining 1 tablespoon oil in now-empty pot over medium-high heat until just

smoking. Brown lamb, about 4 minutes per side; transfer to plate.

3. Add onion to fat left in pot and cook over medium heat until softened, about 5 minutes. Stir in orange zest, ginger, coriander, cinnamon, cayenne, and ⅛ teaspoon pepper and cook until fragrant, about 30 seconds. Stir in wine, scraping up any browned bits. Stir in broth and chickpeas and bring to boil.

4. Nestle lamb into pot along with any accumulated juices. Cover, place pot in oven, and cook until fork slips easily in and out of lamb, about 1 hour.

5. Transfer lamb to cutting board, let cool slightly, then shred into bite-size pieces using 2 forks, discarding excess fat and bones. Strain cooking liquid through fine mesh strainer set over bowl. Return solids and 1½ cups cooking liquid to now-empty pot and bring to simmer over medium heat; discard remaining liquid.

6. Stir in couscous and raisins. Cover, remove pot from heat, and let sit until couscous is tender, about 7 minutes. Add shredded lamb, almonds, and parsley to couscous and gently fluff with fork to combine. Season with salt and pepper to taste and drizzle with extra oil. Serve.

Dinner Meaty Baked Penne

Prep time: 5 minutes | Cook time: 50 minutes | Serves 8

1 pound (454 g) penne pasta

1 pound (454 g) ground beef

1 teaspoon salt

1 (25-ounce) jar marinara sauce

1 (1-pound / 454-g) bag baby spinach, washed

3 cups shredded Mozzarella cheese, divided

1. Bring a large pot of salted water to a boil, add the penne, and cook for 7 minutes. Reserve 2 cups of the pasta water and drain the pasta.

2. Preheat the oven to 350ºF (180ºC).

3. In a large saucepan over medium heat, cook the ground beef and salt. Brown the ground beef for about 5 minutes.

4. Stir in marinara sauce, and 2 cups of pasta water. Let simmer for 5 minutes.

5. Add a handful of spinach at a time into the sauce, and cook for another 3 minutes.

6. To assemble, in a 9-by-13-inch baking dish, add the pasta and pour the pasta sauce over it. Stir in 1½ cups of the Mozzarella cheese. Cover the dish with foil and bake for 20 minutes.

7. After 20 minutes, remove the foil, top with the rest of the Mozzarella, and bake for another 10 minutes. Serve warm.

PER SERVING: Calories: 497; Protein: 31g; Total Carbohydrates: 54g; Sugars: 7g; Fiber: 5g; Total Fat: 18g; Saturated Fat: 8g; Cholesterol: 68mg; Sodium: 1,083mg

Whole-Wheat Fusilli with Chickpea Sauce

Prep time: 15 minutes | Cook time: 15 minutes | Serves 4

¼ cup extra-virgin olive oil

½ large shallot, chopped

5 garlic cloves, thinly sliced

1 (15-ounce / 425-g) can chickpeas, drained and rinsed, reserving ½ cup canning liquid

Pinch red pepper flakes

1 cup whole-grain fusilli pasta

¼ teaspoon salt

⅛ teaspoon freshly ground black pepper

¼ cup shaved fresh Parmesan cheese

¼ cup chopped fresh basil

2 teaspoons dried parsley

1 teaspoon dried oregano

Red pepper flakes

1. In a medium pan, heat the oil over medium heat, and sauté the shallot and garlic for 3 to 5 minutes, until the garlic is golden. Add ¾ of the chickpeas plus 2 tablespoons of liquid from the can, and bring to a simmer.

2. Remove from the heat, transfer into a standard blender, and blend until smooth. At this point, add the remaining chickpeas. Add more reserved chickpea liquid if it becomes thick.

3. Bring a large pot of salted water to a boil and cook pasta until al dente, about 8 minutes. Reserve ½

cup of the pasta water, drain the pasta, and return it to the pot.

4. Add the chickpea sauce to the hot pasta and add up to ¼ cup of the pasta water. You may need to add more pasta water to reach your desired consistency.

5. Place the pasta pot over medium heat and mix occasionally until the sauce thickens. Season with salt and pepper.

6. Serve, garnished with Parmesan, basil, parsley, oregano, and red pepper flakes.

Per Serving (1 cup pasta) Calories: 310; Protein: 10g; Total Carbohydrates: 33g; Sugars: 1g; Fiber: 7g; Total Fat: 17g; Saturated Fat: 3g; Cholesterol: 5mg; Sodium: 243mg

Bow Ties with Zucchini

Prep time: 10 minutes | Cook time: 32 minutes | Serves 4

3 tablespoons extra-virgin olive oil

2 garlic cloves, minced

3 large or 4 medium zucchini, diced

½ teaspoon freshly ground black pepper

¼ teaspoon kosher or sea salt

½ cup 2% milk

¼ teaspoon ground nutmeg

8 ounces (227 g) uncooked farfalle (bow ties) or other small pasta shape

½ cup grated Parmesan or Romano cheese

1 tablespoon freshly squeezed lemon juice

1. In a large skillet over medium heat, heat the oil. Add the garlic and cook for 1 minute, stirring frequently. Add the zucchini, pepper, and salt. Stir

well, cover, and cook for 15 minutes, stirring once or twice.

2. In a small, microwave-safe bowl, warm the milk in the microwave on high for 30 seconds. Stir the milk and nutmeg into the skillet and cook uncovered for another 5 minutes, stirring occasionally.

3. While the zucchini is cooking, in a large stockpot, cook the pasta according to the package directions.

4. Drain the pasta in a colander, saving about 2 tablespoons of pasta water. Add the pasta and pasta water to the skillet. Mix everything together and remove from the heat. Stir in the cheese and lemon juice and serve.

Nutritional Facts Per Serving

Calories: 190g, Total Fat: 10g, Saturated Fat: 3g,Total Carbs: 20 g, Fiber: 3g, Protein: 7g, Sugar: 2g, Sodium : 475mg,Phosphorus:163 mg,Potassium: 149mg,Cholesterol: 18mg,

Linguine with Artichokes and Peas

Prep time: 10 minutes | Cook time: 5 minutes | Serves 4 to 6

1 pound (454 g) linguine

5 cups water, plus extra as needed

1 tablespoon extra-virgin olive oil

1 teaspoon table salt

1 cup jarred whole baby artichokes packed in water, quartered

1 cup frozen peas, thawed

4 ounces (113 g) finely grated Pecorino Romano, plus extra for serving

½ teaspoon pepper

2 teaspoons grated lemon zest

2 tablespoons chopped fresh tarragon

1. Loosely wrap half of pasta in dish towel, then press bundle against corner of counter to break noodles into 6-inch lengths; repeat with remaining pasta.

2. Add pasta, water, oil, and salt to Instant Pot, making sure pasta is completely submerged. Lock lid in place and close pressure release valve. Select high pressure cook function and cook for 4 minutes. Turn off Instant Pot and quick-release pressure. Carefully remove lid, allowing steam to escape away from you.

3. Stir artichokes and peas into pasta, cover, and let sit until heated through, about 3 minutes. Gently stir in Pecorino and pepper until cheese is melted and fully combined, 1 to 2 minutes. Adjust consistency with extra hot water as needed. Stir in lemon zest and tarragon, and season with salt and pepper to taste. Serve, passing extra Pecorino separately.

per serving

Cal 390; Total Fat 8g; Sat Fat 3.5g; Chol 20mg; Sodium 680mg; Total Carbs 59g, Fiber 4g, Total Sugar 3g; Added Sugar 0g; Protein 17g

Rigatoni with Pancetta and Veggie

Prep time: 15 minutes | Cook time: 22 minutes | Serves 4 to 6

4 ounces (113 g) pancetta, chopped fine

1 onion, chopped fine

¼ teaspoon table salt

3 garlic cloves, minced

2 anchovy fillets, rinsed, patted dry, and minced

2 teaspoons fennel seeds, lightly cracked

¼ teaspoon red pepper flakes

1 (28-ounce / 794-g) can diced tomatoes

2 cups chicken broth

1½ cups water

1 pound (454 g) rigatoni

¼ cup grated Pecorino Romano cheese, plus extra for serving

2 tablespoons minced fresh parsley

1. Using highest sauté function, cook pancetta in Instant Pot, stirring often, until browned and fat is well rendered, 6 to 10 minutes. Using slotted spoon, transfer pancetta to paper towel–lined plate; set aside for serving.

2. Add onion and salt to fat left in pot and cook, using highest sauté function, until onion is softened, about 5 minutes. Stir in garlic, anchovies, fennel seeds, and pepper flakes and cook until fragrant, about 1 minute. Stir in tomatoes and their juice, broth, and water, scraping up any browned bits, then stir in pasta.

3. Lock lid in place and close pressure release valve. Select high pressure cook function and cook for 5 minutes. Turn off Instant Pot and quick-release pressure. Carefully remove lid, allowing steam to escape away from you.

4. Stir in Pecorino and season with salt and pepper to taste. Transfer to serving dish and let sit until sauce thickens slightly, about 5 minutes. Sprinkle with parsley and reserved pancetta. Serve, passing extra Pecorino separately.

per serving

Cal 400; Total Fat 8g; Sat Fat 2.5g; Chol 15mg; Sodium 1020mg; Total Carbs 64g, Fiber 6g, Total Sugar 6g; Added Sugar 0g; Protein 17g

Orecchiette with Italian Sausage and Broccoli

Prep time: 10 minutes | Cook time: 13 minutes | Serves 4 to 6

2 tablespoons extra-virgin olive oil, divided

1 pound (454 g) broccoli rabe, trimmed and cut into 1½-inch pieces

¼ teaspoon table salt

8 ounces (227 g) hot or sweet Italian sausage, casings removed

6 garlic cloves, minced

¼ teaspoon red pepper flakes

¼ cup dry white wine

4½ cups chicken broth

1 pound (454 g) orecchiette

2 ounces (57 g) Parmesan cheese, grated, plus extra for serving

1. Using highest sauté function, heat 1 tablespoon oil in Instant Pot until shimmering. Add broccoli rabe and salt, partially cover, and cook, stirring occasionally, until broccoli rabe is softened, 3 to 5 minutes. Using slotted spoon, transfer broccoli rabe to bowl; set aside.

2. Add sausage and remaining 1 tablespoon oil to now-empty pot. Using highest sauté function, cook sausage, breaking up meat with wooden spoon, until lightly browned, about 5 minutes. Stir in garlic and pepper flakes and cook until fragrant, about 30 seconds. Stir in wine, scraping up any browned bits, then stir in broth and pasta.

3. Lock lid in place and close pressure release valve. Select high pressure cook function and cook for 4

minutes. Turn off Instant Pot and quick-release pressure. Carefully remove lid, allowing steam to escape away from you.

4. Stir broccoli rabe and any accumulated juices and Parmesan into pasta. Season with salt and pepper to taste. Serve, passing extra Parmesan separately.

per serving

Cal 440; Total Fat 13g; Sat Fat 3.5g; Chol 20mg; Sodium 930mg; Total Carbs 59g, Fiber 1g, Total Sugar 2g; Added Sugar 0g; Protein 22g

Orzo with Shrimp and Feta Cheese

Prep time: 15 minutes | Cook time: 13 minutes | Serves 4 to 6

1 pound (454 g) large shrimp, peeled and deveined

1 tablespoon grated lemon zest plus 1 tablespoon juice

¼ teaspoon table salt

¼ teaspoon pepper

2 tablespoons extra-virgin olive oil, plus extra for serving

1 onion, chopped fine

2 garlic cloves, minced

2 cups orzo

2 cups chicken broth, plus extra as needed

1¼ cups water

½ cup pitted kalamata olives, chopped coarse

1 ounce (28 g) Feta cheese, crumbled, plus extra for serving

1 tablespoon chopped fresh dill

1. Toss shrimp with lemon zest, salt, and pepper in bowl; refrigerate until ready to use.

2. Using highest sauté function, heat oil in Instant Pot until shimmering. Add onion and cook until softened, about 5 minutes. Stir in garlic and cook until fragrant, about 30 seconds. Add orzo and cook, stirring frequently, until orzo is coated with oil and lightly browned, about 5 minutes. Stir in broth and water, scraping up any browned bits.

3. Lock lid in place and close pressure release valve. Select high pressure cook function and cook for 2 minutes. Turn off Instant Pot and quick-release

pressure. Carefully remove lid, allowing steam to escape away from you.

4. Stir shrimp, olives, and Feta into orzo. Cover and let sit until shrimp are opaque throughout, 5 to 7 minutes. Adjust consistency with extra hot broth as needed. Stir in dill and lemon juice, and season with salt and pepper to taste. Sprinkle individual portions with extra Feta and drizzle with extra oil before serving.

per serving

Cal 320; Total Fat 8g; Sat Fat 2g; Chol 75mg; Sodium 670mg; Total Carbs 46g, Fiber 2g, Total Sugar 4g; Added Sugar 0g; Protein 18g

Herbed Barley with Nuts

Prep time: 10 minutes | Cook time: 25 minutes | Serves 4

2 tablespoons olive oil

½ cup diced onion

½ cup diced celery

1 carrot, peeled and diced

3 cups water or chicken broth

1 cup barley

1 bay leaf

½ teaspoon thyme

½ teaspoon rosemary

¼ cup walnuts or pine nuts

Sea salt and freshly ground pepper, to taste

1. Heat the olive oil in a medium saucepan over medium-high heat. Sauté the onion, celery, and carrot over medium heat until they are tender.

2. Add the water or chicken broth, barley, and seasonings, and bring to a boil. Reduce the heat and simmer for 25 minutes, or until tender.

3. Stir in the nuts and season to taste.

Brown Rice and Lentils

Prep time: 10 minutes | Cook time: 1 hour | Serves 4

2 cups green or brown lentils

1 cup brown rice

5 cups water or chicken stock

½ teaspoon sea salt

½ teaspoon freshly ground pepper

½ teaspoon dried thyme

¼ cup olive oil

3 onions, peeled and sliced

1. Place the lentils and rice in a large saucepan with water or chicken stock. Bring to a boil, cover, and simmer for 20 to 25 minutes, or until almost tender.

2. Add the seasonings and cook an additional 20 to 30 minutes, or until the rice is tender and the water is absorbed.

3. In another saucepan, heat the olive oil over medium heat. Add the onions and cook very slowly, stirring frequently, until the onions become browned and caramelized, about 20 minutes.

4. To serve, ladle the lentils and rice into bowls and top with the caramelized onions.

Brown Rice Pilaf

Prep time: 10 minutes | Cook time: 23 minutes | Serves 6

2 tablespoons olive oil

1 medium onion, diced

¼ cup pine nuts

1½ cups long-grain brown rice

2 ½ cups hot chicken stock

1 cinnamon stick

¼ cup raisins

Sea salt and freshly ground pepper, to taste

1. Heat the olive oil in a large saucepan over medium heat.

2. Sauté the onions and pine nuts for 6 to 8 minutes, or until the pine nuts are golden and the onion is translucent.

3. Add the rice and sauté for 2 minutes until lightly browned. Pour the chicken stock into the pan and bring to a boil.

4. Add the cinnamon and raisins.

5. Lower the heat, cover the pan, and simmer for 15 to 20 minutes, or until the rice is tender and the liquid is absorbed.

6. Remove from the heat and fluff with a fork. Season and serve.

Wild Parmesan Mushroom Risotto

Prep time: 10 minutes | Cook time: 23 minutes | Serves 6

2 ounces (57 g) dried porcini mushrooms

5 cups chicken stock

2 tablespoons olive oil

1 small onion, minced

2 cups brown rice

½ cup freshly grated, low-fat Parmesan cheese

Sea salt and freshly ground pepper, to taste

1. Place the mushrooms in a bowl and cover them with hot water. Set them aside for 30 minutes. Drain them, reserving the liquid, and wash them.

2. Strain the liquid through a sieve lined with cheesecloth. Add the liquid to the chicken stock.

3. Heat the chicken stock and mushroom liquid in a small saucepan. When simmering, turn heat to lowest setting.

4. Heat the olive oil in a large saucepan over medium heat. Add the onion and sauté for 3 to 5 minutes, or until tender. Stir in the rice and mushrooms and ¾ cup of the stock.

5. Continue cooking the rice, stirring almost constantly, and adding more liquid, a ladleful at a time, as soon as the rice absorbs the liquid. There should always be some liquid visible in the pan.

6. Cook, adding liquid every few minutes, until the rice is tender, with a slightly firm center, 20 to 30 minutes.

7. Remove from the heat, and stir in the Parmesan cheese, a spoonful at a time.

8. Season to taste and serve.

Basmati Rice with Currant and Almond

Prep time: 10 minutes | Cook time: 24 minutes | Serves 4 to 6

1 tablespoon extra-virgin olive oil

1 small onion, chopped fine

Salt and pepper, to taste

1½ cups basmati rice, rinsed

2 garlic cloves, minced

½ teaspoon ground turmeric

¼ teaspoon ground cinnamon

2¼ cups water

¼ cup currants

¼ cup sliced almonds, toasted

1. Heat oil in large saucepan over medium heat until shimmering. Add onion and ¼ teaspoon salt and cook until softened, about 5 minutes. Add rice, garlic, turmeric, and cinnamon and cook, stirring frequently, until grain edges begin to turn translucent, about 3 minutes.

2. Stir in water and bring to simmer. Reduce heat to low, cover, and simmer gently until rice is tender and water is absorbed, 16 to 18 minutes.

3. Off heat, sprinkle currants over pilaf. Cover, laying clean dish towel underneath lid, and let pilaf sit for 10 minutes. Add almonds to pilaf and fluff gently with fork to combine. Season with salt and pepper to taste. Serve.

Basmati Rice with Pomegranate and Cilantro

Prep time: 15 minutes | Cook time: 34 minutes | Serves 8 to 10

1 (2-pound / 907-g) head cauliflower, cored and cut into ¾-inch florets

¼ cup extra-virgin olive oil

Salt and pepper, to taste

½ teaspoon ground cumin

1 onion, chopped coarse

1½ cups basmati rice, rinsed

4 garlic cloves, minced

½ teaspoon ground cinnamon

½ teaspoon ground turmeric

2¼ cups water

½ cup pomegranate seeds

2 tablespoons chopped fresh cilantro

2 tablespoons chopped fresh mint

1. Adjust oven rack to lowest position and heat oven to 475ºF (245ºC). Toss cauliflower with 2 tablespoons oil, ½ teaspoon salt, ½ teaspoon pepper, and ¼ teaspoon cumin. Arrange cauliflower in single layer in rimmed baking sheet and roast until just tender, 10 to 15 minutes; set aside.

2. Heat remaining 2 tablespoons oil in large saucepan over medium heat until shimmering. Add onion and ¼ teaspoon salt and cook until softened and lightly browned, 5 to 7 minutes. Add rice, garlic, cinnamon, turmeric, and remaining ¼ teaspoon cumin and cook, stirring frequently, until grain edges begin to turn translucent, about 3 minutes.

3. Stir in water and bring to simmer. Reduce heat to low, cover, and simmer gently until rice is tender and water is absorbed, 16 to 18 minutes.

4. Off heat, lay clean dish towel underneath lid and let pilaf sit for 10 minutes. Add roasted cauliflower to pilaf and fluff gently with fork to combine. Season with salt and pepper to taste. Transfer to serving platter and sprinkle with pomegranate seeds, cilantro, and mint. Serve.

Basmati Rice and Vermicelli Pasta Pilaf

Prep time: 10 minutes | Cook time: 20 minutes | Serves 4 to 6

1½ cups basmati rice

3 tablespoons extra-virgin olive oil

2 ounces (57 g) vermicelli pasta, broken into 1-inch lengths

1 onion, chopped fine

1 garlic clove, minced

Salt and pepper, to taste

2½ cups chicken or vegetable broth

3 tablespoons minced fresh parsley

1. Place rice in medium bowl and cover with hot tap water by 2 inches; let stand for 15 minutes.

2. Using your hands, gently swish grains to release excess starch. Carefully pour off water, leaving rice

in bowl. Add cold tap water to rice and pour off water. Repeat adding and pouring off cold water 4 to 5 times, until water runs almost clear. Drain rice in fine-mesh strainer.

3. Heat oil in large saucepan over medium heat until shimmering. Add pasta and cook, stirring occasionally, until browned, about 3 minutes. Add onion and garlic and cook, stirring occasionally, until onion is softened but not browned, about 4 minutes. Add rice and cook, stirring occasionally, until edges of rice begin to turn translucent, about 3 minutes. Add broth and 1¼ teaspoons salt and bring to boil. Reduce heat to low, cover, and simmer gently until rice and pasta are tender and broth is absorbed, about 10 minutes. Off heat, lay clean dish towel underneath lid and let pilaf sit for 10 minutes. Add parsley to pilaf and fluff gently with fork to combine. Season with salt and pepper to taste. Serve.

Brown Rice with Red Pepper and Onion

Prep time: 10 minutes | Cook time: 1½ hours | Serves 4 to 6

4 teaspoons extra-virgin olive oil

2 onions, chopped fine

Salt and pepper, to taste

2¼ cups water

1 cup chicken or vegetable broth

1½ cups long-grain brown rice, rinsed

¾ cup jarred roasted red peppers, rinsed, patted dry, and chopped

½ cup minced fresh parsley

Grated Parmesan cheese

Lemon wedges

1. Adjust oven rack to middle position and heat oven to 375ºF (190ºC). Heat oil in Dutch oven over medium heat until shimmering. Add onions and 1 teaspoon salt and cook, stirring occasionally, until softened and well browned, 12 to 14 minutes.

2. Stir in water and broth and bring to boil. Stir in rice, cover, and transfer pot to oven. Bake until rice is tender and liquid is absorbed, 65 to 70 minutes.

3. Remove pot from oven. Sprinkle red peppers over rice, cover, and let sit for 5 minutes. Add parsley to rice and fluff gently with fork to combine. Season with salt and pepper to taste. Serve with grated Parmesan and lemon wedges.

Rice with Oranges, Green Olives, and Almonds

Prep time: 10 minutes | Cook time: 20 minutes | Serves 4 to 6

1½ cups basmati rice

Salt and pepper, to taste

2 oranges, plus ¼ teaspoon grated orange zest plus 1 tablespoon juice

2 tablespoons extra-virgin olive oil

2 teaspoons sherry vinegar

1 small garlic clove, minced

⅓ cup large pitted brine-cured green olives, chopped

⅓ cup slivered almonds, toasted

2 tablespoons minced fresh oregano

1. Bring 4 quarts water to boil in Dutch oven. Meanwhile, toast rice in 12-inch skillet over medium heat until faintly fragrant and some grains turn opaque, 5 to 8 minutes. Add rice and 1½ teaspoons salt to boiling water and cook, stirring occasionally, until rice is tender but not soft, about 15 minutes. Drain rice, spread onto rimmed baking sheet, and let cool completely, about 15 minutes.

2. Cut away peel and pith from oranges. Holding fruit over bowl, use paring knife to slice between membranes to release segments. Whisk oil, vinegar, garlic, orange zest and juice, 1 teaspoon salt, and ½ teaspoon pepper together in large bowl. Add rice, orange segments, olives, almonds, and oregano, gently toss to combine, and let sit for 20 minutes. Serve.

Rice Salad with Asparagus and Parsley

Prep time: 10 minutes | Cook time: 30 minutes | Serves 4 to 6

1½ cups long-grain brown rice

Salt and pepper, to taste

1 teaspoon grated lemon zest plus 3 tablespoons juice

3½ tablespoons extra-virgin olive oil

1 pound (454 g) asparagus, trimmed and cut into 1-inch lengths

1 shallot, minced

2 ounces (57 g) Goat cheese, crumbled

¼ cup slivered almonds, toasted

¼ cup minced fresh parsley

1. Bring 4 quarts water to boil in Dutch oven. Add rice and 1½ teaspoons salt and cook, stirring occasionally, until rice is tender, 25 to 30 minutes.

Drain rice, spread onto rimmed baking sheet, and drizzle with 1 tablespoon lemon juice. Let cool completely, about 15 minutes.

2. Heat 1 tablespoon oil in 12-inch skillet over high heat until just smoking. Add asparagus, ¼ teaspoon salt, and ¼ teaspoon pepper and cook, stirring occasionally, until asparagus is browned and crisp-tender, about 4 minutes; transfer to plate and let cool slightly.

3. Whisk remaining 2½ tablespoons oil, lemon zest and remaining 2 tablespoons juice, shallot, ½ teaspoon salt, and ½ teaspoon pepper together in large bowl. Add rice, asparagus, 2 tablespoons Goat cheese, 3 tablespoons almonds, and 3 tablespoons parsley. Gently toss to combine and let sit for 10 minutes. Season with salt and pepper to taste. Transfer to serving platter and sprinkle with remaining 2 tablespoons Goat cheese, remaining 1 tablespoon almonds, and remaining 1 tablespoon parsley. Serve.

Polenta with Parmesan Cheese

Prep time: 10 minutes | Cook time: 31 minutes | Serves 4 to 6

7½ cups water

Salt and pepper, to taste

Pinch baking soda

1½ cups coarse-ground cornmeal

2 ounces (57 g) Parmesan cheese, grated, plus extra for serving

2 tablespoons extra-virgin olive oil

1. Bring water to boil in large saucepan over medium-high heat. Stir in 1½ teaspoons salt and baking soda. Slowly pour cornmeal into water in steady stream while stirring back and forth with wooden spoon or rubber spatula. Bring mixture to boil, stirring constantly, about 1 minute. Reduce heat to lowest setting and cover.

2. After 5 minutes, whisk polenta to smooth out any lumps that may have formed, about 15 seconds. (Make sure to scrape down sides and bottom of saucepan.) Cover and continue to cook, without stirring, until polenta grains are tender but slightly al dente, about 25 minutes longer. (Polenta should be loose and barely hold its shape; it will continue to thicken as it cools.)

3. Off heat, stir in Parmesan and oil and season with pepper to taste. Cover and let sit for 5 minutes. Serve, passing extra Parmesan separately.

Barley Pilaf with Parsley and Chives

Prep time: 10 minutes | Cook time: 9 minutes | Serves 4 to 6

3 tablespoons extra-virgin olive oil

1 small onion, chopped fine

Salt and pepper, to taste

1½ cups pearl barley, rinsed

2 garlic cloves, minced

1½ teaspoons minced fresh thyme or ½ teaspoon dried

2½ cups water

¼ cup minced fresh parsley

2 tablespoons minced fresh chives

1½ teaspoons lemon juice

1. Heat oil in large saucepan over medium heat until shimmering. Add onion and ½ teaspoon salt and cook until softened, about 5 minutes. Stir in barley, garlic, and thyme and cook, stirring frequently, until barley is lightly toasted and fragrant, about 3 minutes.

2. Stir in water and bring to simmer. Reduce heat to low, cover, and simmer until barley is tender and water is absorbed, 20 to 40 minutes.

3. Off heat, lay clean dish towel underneath lid and let pilaf sit for 10 minutes. Add parsley, chives, and lemon juice to pilaf and fluff gently with fork to combine. Season with salt and pepper to taste. Serve.

Barley with Carrots, Snow Peas, and Sunflower Seeds

Prep time: 15 minutes | Cook time: 30 minutes | Serves 4

½ cup plain yogurt

1½ teaspoons grated lemon zest plus 1½ tablespoons juice

1½ tablespoons minced fresh mint

Salt and pepper, to taste

1 cup pearl barley

5 carrots, peeled

3 tablespoons extra-virgin olive oil

¾ teaspoon ground coriander

8 ounces (227 g) snow peas, strings removed, halved lengthwise

2/3 cup raw sunflower seeds

½ teaspoon ground cumin

⅛ teaspoon ground cardamom

1. Whisk yogurt, ½ teaspoon lemon zest and 1½ teaspoons juice, 1½ teaspoons mint, ¼ teaspoon

salt, and ⅛ teaspoon pepper together in small bowl; cover and refrigerate until ready to serve.

2. Bring 4 quarts water to boil in Dutch oven. Add barley and 1 tablespoon salt, return to boil, and cook until tender, 20 to 40 minutes. Drain barley, return to now-empty pot, and cover to keep warm.

3. Meanwhile, halve carrots crosswise, then halve or quarter lengthwise to create uniformly sized pieces. Heat 1 tablespoon oil in 12-inch skillet over medium-high heat until just smoking. Add carrots and ½ teaspoon coriander and cook, stirring occasionally, until lightly charred and just tender, 5 to 7 minutes. Add snow peas and cook, stirring occasionally, until spotty brown, 3 to 5 minutes; transfer to plate.

4. Heat 1½ teaspoons oil in now-empty skillet over medium heat until shimmering. Add sunflower seeds, cumin, cardamom, remaining ¼ teaspoon coriander, and ¼ teaspoon salt. Cook, stirring constantly, until seeds are toasted, about 2 minutes; transfer to small bowl.

5. Whisk remaining 1 teaspoon lemon zest and 1 tablespoon juice, remaining 1 tablespoon mint, and remaining 1½ tablespoons oil together in large bowl. Add barley and carrot–snow pea mixture and gently toss to combine. Season with salt and pepper to taste. Serve, topping individual portions with spiced sunflower seeds and drizzling with yogurt sauce.

Barley Risotto with Parmesan cheese

Prep time: 10 minutes | Cook time: 1 hour | Serves 4 to 6

4 cups chicken or vegetable broth

4 cups water

2 tablespoons extra-virgin olive oil

1 onion, chopped fine

1 carrot, peeled and chopped fine

1½ cups pearl barley

1 cup dry white wine

1 teaspoon minced fresh thyme or ¼ teaspoon dried

2 ounces (57 g) Parmesan cheese, grated

Salt and pepper, to taste

1. Bring broth and water to simmer in medium saucepan. Reduce heat to low and cover to keep warm.

2. Heat 1 tablespoon oil in Dutch oven over medium heat until shimmering. Add onion and carrot and cook until softened, 5 to 7 minutes. Add barley and cook, stirring often, until lightly toasted and aromatic, about 4 minutes.

3. Add wine and cook, stirring frequently, until fully absorbed, about 2 minutes. Stir in 3 cups warm broth and thyme, bring to simmer, and cook, stirring occasionally, until liquid is absorbed and bottom of pot is dry, 22 to 25 minutes. Stir in 2 cups warm broth, bring to simmer, and cook, stirring occasionally, until liquid is absorbed and bottom of pot is dry, 15 to 18 minutes.

4. Continue to cook risotto, stirring often and adding warm broth as needed to prevent pot bottom from becoming dry, until barley is cooked through but still somewhat firm in center, 15 to 20 minutes. Off heat, adjust consistency with remaining warm broth as needed (you may have broth left over). Stir in Parmesan and remaining 1 tablespoon oil and season with salt and pepper to taste. Serve.

Farro with Lemony Parsley and Mint

Prep time: 10 minutes | Cook time: 18 minutes | Serves 4 to 6

1½ cups whole farro

Salt and pepper, to taste

3 tablespoons extra-virgin olive oil

1 onion, chopped fine

1 garlic clove, minced

¼ cup chopped fresh parsley

¼ cup chopped fresh mint

1 tablespoon lemon juice

1. Bring 4 quarts water to boil in Dutch oven. Add farro and 1 tablespoon salt, return to boil, and cook until grains are tender with slight chew, 15 to 30 minutes. Drain farro, return to now-empty pot, and cover to keep warm.

2. Heat 2 tablespoons oil in 12-inch skillet over medium heat until shimmering. Add onion and ¼ teaspoon salt and cook until softened, about 5 minutes. Stir in garlic and cook until fragrant, about 30 seconds.

3. Add remaining 1 tablespoon oil and farro and cook, stirring frequently, until heated through, about 2 minutes. Off heat, stir in parsley, mint, and lemon juice. Season with salt and pepper to taste. Serve.

Warm Farro with Mushrooms and Shallot

Prep time: 10 minutes | Cook time: 25 minutes | Serves 4 to 6

1½ cups whole farro

Salt and pepper, to taste

3 tablespoons extra-virgin olive oil

12 ounces (340 g) cremini mushrooms, trimmed and chopped coarse

1 shallot, minced

1½ teaspoons minced fresh thyme or ½ teaspoon dried

3 tablespoons dry sherry

3 tablespoons minced fresh parsley

1½ teaspoons sherry vinegar, plus extra for serving

1. Bring 4 quarts water to boil in Dutch oven. Add farro and 1 tablespoon salt, return to boil, and cook until grains are tender with slight chew, 15 to 30 minutes. Drain farro, return to now-empty pot, and cover to keep warm.

2. Heat 2 tablespoons oil in 12-inch skillet over medium heat until shimmering. Add mushrooms, shallot, thyme, and ¼ teaspoon salt and cook, stirring occasionally, until moisture has evaporated and vegetables start to brown, 8 to 10 minutes. Stir in sherry and cook, scraping up any browned bits, until skillet is almost dry.

3. Add remaining 1 tablespoon oil and farro and cook, stirring frequently, until heated through, about 2 minutes. Off heat, stir in parsley and vinegar. Season with salt, pepper, and extra vinegar to taste and serve.

Farro with Asparagu, Snap Peas, and Tomato

Prep time: 10 minutes | Cook time: 18 minutes | Serves 4 to 6

6 ounces (170 g) asparagus, trimmed and cut into 1-inch lengths

6 ounces (170 g) sugar snap peas, strings removed, cut into 1-inch lengths

Salt and pepper, to taste

1½ cups whole farro

3 tablespoons extra-virgin olive oil

2 tablespoons lemon juice

2 tablespoons minced shallot

1 teaspoon Dijon mustard

6 ounces (170 g) cherry tomatoes, halved

3 tablespoons chopped fresh dill

2 ounces (57 g) Feta cheese, crumbled

1. Bring 4 quarts water to boil in Dutch oven. Add asparagus, snap peas, and 1 tablespoon salt and cook until crisp-tender, about 3 minutes. Using slotted spoon, transfer vegetables to large plate and let cool completely, about 15 minutes.

2. Add farro to water, return to boil, and cook until grains are tender with slight chew, 15 to 30 minutes. Drain farro, spread in rimmed baking sheet, and let cool completely, about 15 minutes.

3. Whisk oil, lemon juice, shallot, mustard, ¼ teaspoon salt, and ¼ teaspoon pepper together in large bowl. Add vegetables, farro, tomatoes, dill, and ¼ cup Feta and toss gently to combine. Season with salt and pepper to taste. Transfer to serving platter and sprinkle with remaining ¼ cup Feta. Serve.

Farro with English Cucumber, Yogurt, and Mint

Prep time: 10 minutes | Cook time: 15 minutes | Serves 4 to 6

1½ cups whole farro

Salt and pepper, to taste

3 tablespoons extra-virgin olive oil

2 tablespoons lemon juice

2 tablespoons minced shallot

2 tablespoons plain Greek yogurt

1 English cucumber, halved lengthwise, seeded, and cut into ¼-inch pieces

6 ounces (170 g) cherry tomatoes, halved

1 cup baby arugula

3 tablespoons chopped fresh mint

1. Bring 4 quarts water to boil in Dutch oven. Add farro and 1 tablespoon salt, return to boil, and cook until grains are tender with slight chew, 15 to 30 minutes. Drain farro, spread in rimmed baking sheet, and let cool completely, about 15 minutes.

2. Whisk oil, lemon juice, shallot, yogurt, ¼ teaspoon salt, and ¼ teaspoon pepper together in large bowl. Add farro, cucumber, tomatoes, arugula, and mint and toss gently to combine. Season with salt and pepper to taste. Serve.

Farrotto with Parmesan Cheese

Prep time: 10 minutes | Cook time: 39 minutes | Serves 6

1½ cups whole farro

3 cups chicken or vegetable broth

3 cups water

3 tablespoons extra-virgin olive oil

½ onion, chopped fine

1 garlic clove, minced

2 teaspoons minced fresh thyme

Salt and pepper, to taste

2 ounces (57 g) Parmesan cheese, grated

2 tablespoons minced fresh parsley

2 teaspoons lemon juice

1. Pulse farro in blender until about half of grains are broken into smaller pieces, about 6 pulses.

2. Bring broth and water to boil in medium saucepan over high heat. Reduce heat to low, cover, and keep warm.

3. Heat 2 tablespoons oil in Dutch oven over medium-low heat. Add onion and cook until softened, about 5 minutes. Stir in garlic and cook until fragrant, about 30 seconds. Add farro and cook, stirring frequently, until grains are lightly toasted, about 3 minutes.

4. Stir 5 cups warm broth mixture into farro mixture, reduce heat to low, cover, and cook until almost all liquid has been absorbed and farro is just al dente, about 25 minutes, stirring twice during cooking.

5. Add thyme, 1 teaspoon salt, and ¾ teaspoon pepper and cook, stirring constantly, until farro becomes creamy, about 5 minutes. Off heat, stir in Parmesan, parsley, lemon juice, and remaining 1 tablespoon oil. Adjust consistency with remaining warm broth mixture as needed (you may have broth left over). Season with salt and pepper to taste. Serve.

Oregano Wheat Berries with Veggie

Prep time: 10 minutes | Cook time: 1¼ hours | Serves 4 to 6

1½ cups wheat berries

Salt and pepper, to taste

2 tablespoons extra-virgin olive oil

3 tablespoons red wine vinegar

1 garlic clove, minced

1 tablespoon grated lemon zest

1 tablespoon minced fresh oregano or 1½ teaspoons dried

1 zucchini, cut into ½-inch pieces

1 red onion, chopped

1 red bell pepper, stemmed, seeded, and cut into ½-inch pieces

1. Bring 4 quarts water to boil in Dutch oven. Add wheat berries and 1½ teaspoons salt, return to boil, and cook until tender but still chewy, 60 to 70 minutes.

2. Meanwhile, whisk 1 tablespoon oil, vinegar, garlic, lemon zest, and oregano together in large bowl. Drain wheat berries, add to bowl with dressing, and toss gently to coat.

3. Heat 2 teaspoons oil in 12-inch nonstick skillet over medium-high heat until just smoking. Add zucchini and ¼ teaspoon salt and cook, stirring occasionally, until deep golden brown and beginning to char in spots, 6 to 8 minutes; transfer to bowl with wheat berries.

4. Return now-empty skillet to medium-high heat and add remaining 1 teaspoon oil, onion, bell pepper, and ¼ teaspoon salt. Cook, stirring occasionally, until onion is charred at edges and pepper skin is charred and blistered, 8 to 10 minutes. Add wheat berry–zucchini mixture and cook, stirring frequently, until heated through, about 2 minutes. Season with salt and pepper to taste. Serve.

Wheat Berry Salad with Orange and Veggie

Prep time: 15 minutes | Cook time: 1 hour | Serves 4 to 6

1½ cups wheat berries

Salt and pepper, to taste

1 orange

3 tablespoons red wine vinegar

1½ tablespoons Dijon mustard

1 small shallot, minced

1 garlic clove, minced

⅛ teaspoon grated orange zest

1½ teaspoons honey

2 tablespoons extra-virgin olive oil

3 carrots, peeled and shredded

1 tablespoon minced fresh tarragon

1. Bring 4 quarts water to boil in Dutch oven. Add wheat berries and 1½ teaspoons salt, return to

boil, and cook until tender but still chewy, 60 to 70 minutes. Drain wheat berries, spread in rimmed baking sheet, and let cool completely, about 15 minutes.

2. Cut away peel and pith from orange. Quarter orange, then slice crosswise into ¼-inch-thick pieces. Whisk vinegar, mustard, shallot, garlic, orange zest, honey, and ¼ teaspoon salt together in large bowl until combined. Whisking constantly, slowly drizzle in oil. Add wheat berries, carrots, tarragon, and orange pieces and gently toss to coat. Season with salt and pepper to taste. Serve.

Wheat Berry Salad with Figs and Nuts

Prep time: 10 minutes | Cook time: 1 hour | Serves 4 to 6

1½ cups wheat berries

Salt and pepper, to taste

2 tablespoons balsamic vinegar

1 small shallot, minced

1 teaspoon Dijon mustard

1 teaspoon honey

3 tablespoons extra-virgin olive oil

8 ounces (227 g) figs, cut into ½-inch pieces

½ cup fresh parsley leaves

¼ cup pine nuts, toasted

2 ounces (57 g) Goat cheese, crumbled

1. Bring 4 quarts water to boil in Dutch oven. Add wheat berries and 1½ teaspoons salt, return to boil, and cook until tender but still chewy, 60 to 70 minutes. Drain wheat berries, spread onto rimmed

baking sheet, and let cool completely, about 15 minutes.

2. Whisk vinegar, shallot, mustard, honey, ¼ teaspoon salt, and ¼ teaspoon pepper together in large bowl. Whisking constantly, slowly drizzle in oil. Add wheat berries, figs, parsley, and pine nuts and toss gently to combine. Season with salt and pepper to taste. Transfer to serving platter and sprinkle with Goat cheese. Serve.

Mediterranean Lentils and Brown Rice

Prep time: 15 minutes | Cook time: 23 minutes | Serves 4

2¼ cups low-sodium or no-salt-added vegetable broth

½ cup uncooked brown or green lentils

½ cup uncooked instant brown rice

½ cup diced carrots

½ cup diced celery

1 (2¼-ounce / 64-g) can sliced olives, drained

¼ cup diced red onion

¼ cup chopped fresh curly-leaf parsley

1½ tablespoons extra-virgin olive oil

1 tablespoon freshly squeezed lemon juice

1 garlic clove, minced

¼ teaspoon kosher or sea salt

¼ teaspoon freshly ground black pepper

1. In a medium saucepan over high heat, bring the broth and lentils to a boil, cover, and lower the heat to medium-low. Cook for 8 minutes.

2. Raise the heat to medium, and stir in the rice. Cover the pot and cook the mixture for 15 minutes, or until the liquid is absorbed. Remove the pot from the heat and let it sit, covered, for 1 minute, then stir.

3. While the lentils and rice are cooking, mix together the carrots, celery, olives, onion, and parsley in a large serving bowl.

4. In a small bowl, whisk together the oil, lemon juice, garlic, salt, and pepper. Set aside.

5. When the lentils and rice are cooked, add them to the serving bowl. Pour the dressing on top, and mix everything together. Serve warm or cold, or store in a sealed container in the refrigerator for up to 7 days.

Nutritional Facts Per Serving
Calories: 170g, Total Fat: 6g, Saturated Fat: 1g,Total Carbs: 25 g, Fiber: 3g, Protein: 5g, Sugar: 3g, Sodium : 566mg,Phosphorus:98 mg,Potassium: 227mg,Cholesterol: 2mg,

Wild Mushroom Farrotto with Parmesan

Prep time: 15 minutes | Cook time: 7 minutes | Serves 4

1½ cups whole farro

3 tablespoons extra-virgin olive oil, divided, plus extra for drizzling

12 ounces (340 g) cremini or white mushrooms, trimmed and sliced thin

½ onion, chopped fine

½ teaspoon table salt

¼ teaspoon pepper

1 garlic clove, minced

¼ ounce (7 g) dried porcini mushrooms, rinsed and chopped fine

2 teaspoons minced fresh thyme or ½ teaspoon dried

¼ cup dry white wine

2½ cups chicken or vegetable broth, plus extra as needed

2 ounces (57 g) Parmesan cheese, grated, plus extra for serving

2 teaspoons lemon juice

½ cup chopped fresh parsley

1. Pulse farro in blender until about half of grains are broken into smaller pieces, about 6 pulses.

2. Using highest sauté function, heat 2 tablespoons oil in Instant Pot until shimmering. Add cremini mushrooms, onion, salt, and pepper, partially cover, and cook until mushrooms are softened and have released their liquid, about 5 minutes. Stir in farro, garlic, porcini mushrooms, and thyme and cook until fragrant, about 1 minute. Stir in wine and cook until nearly evaporated, about 30 seconds. Stir in broth.

3. Lock lid in place and close pressure release valve. Select high pressure cook function and cook for 12

minutes. Turn off Instant Pot and quick-release pressure. Carefully remove lid, allowing steam to escape away from you.

4. If necessary adjust consistency with extra hot broth, or continue to cook farrotto, using highest sauté function, stirring frequently, until proper consistency is achieved. (Farrotto should be slightly thickened, and spoon dragged along bottom of multicooker should leave trail that quickly fills in.) Add Parmesan and remaining 1 tablespoon oil and stir vigorously until farrotto becomes creamy. Stir in lemon juice and season with salt and pepper to taste. Sprinkle individual portions with parsley and extra Parmesan, and drizzle with extra oil before serving.

per serving

Cal 280; Total Fat 10g; Sat Fat 2.5g; Chol 5mg; Sodium 630mg; Total Carbs 35g, Fiber 4g, Total Sugar 2g; Added Sugar 0g; Protein 13g

Barley Pilaf with Mushrooms

Prep time: 10 minutes | Cook time: 35 minutes | Serves 4

Olive oil cooking spray

2 tablespoons olive oil

8 ounces (227 g) button mushrooms, diced

½ yellow onion, diced

2 garlic cloves, minced

1 cup pearl barley

2 cups vegetable broth

1 tablespoon fresh thyme, chopped

½ teaspoon salt

¼ teaspoon smoked paprika

Fresh parsley, for garnish

1. Preheat the air fryer to 380ºF (193ºC). Lightly coat the inside of a 5-cup capacity casserole dish with olive oil cooking spray. (The shape of the casserole dish will depend upon the size of the air fryer, but it needs to be able to hold at least 5 cups.)

2. In a large skillet, heat the olive oil over medium heat. Add the mushrooms and onion and cook,

stirring occasionally, for 5 minutes, or until the mushrooms begin to brown.

3. Add the garlic and cook for an additional 2 minutes. Transfer the vegetables to a large bowl.

4. Add the barley, broth, thyme, salt, and paprika.

5. Pour the barley-and-vegetable mixture into the prepared casserole dish, and place the dish into the air fryer. Bake for 15 minutes.

6. Stir the barley mixture. Reduce the heat to 360ºF (182ºC), then return the barley to the air fryer and bake for 15 minutes more.

7. Remove from the air fryer and let sit for 5 minutes before fluffing with a fork and topping with fresh parsley.

PER SERVING: Calories: 263; Total Fat: 8g; Saturated Fat: 1g; Protein: 7g; Total Carbohydrates: 44g; Fiber: 9g; Sugar: 3g; Cholesterol: 0mg

Moroccan-Style Brown Rice and Chickpea

Prep time: 15 minutes | Cook time: 45 minutes | Serves 6

Olive oil cooking spray

1 cup long-grain brown rice

2¼ cups chicken stock

1 (15½-ounce / 439-g) can chickpeas, drained and rinsed

½ cup diced carrot

½ cup green peas

1 teaspoon ground cumin

½ teaspoon ground turmeric

½ teaspoon ground ginger

½ teaspoon onion powder

½ teaspoon salt

¼ teaspoon ground cinnamon

¼ teaspoon garlic powder

¼ teaspoon black pepper

Fresh parsley, for garnish

1. Preheat the air fryer to 380ºF (193ºC). Lightly coat the inside of a 5-cup capacity casserole dish with olive oil cooking spray. (The shape of the casserole dish will depend upon the size of the air fryer, but it needs to be able to hold at least 5 cups.)

2. In the casserole dish, combine the rice, stock, chickpeas, carrot, peas, cumin, turmeric, ginger, onion powder, salt, cinnamon, garlic powder, and black pepper. Stir well to combine.

3. Cover loosely with aluminum foil.

4. Place the covered casserole dish into the air fryer and bake for 20 minutes. Remove from the air fryer and stir well.

5. Place the casserole back into the air fryer, uncovered, and bake for 25 minutes more.

6. Fluff with a spoon and sprinkle with fresh chopped parsley before serving.

PER SERVING: Calories: 204; Total Fat: 2g; Saturated Fat: 0g; Protein: 7g; Total Carbohydrates: 40g; Fiber: 5g; Sugar: 4g; Cholesterol: 0mg

Buckwheat Groats with Root Vegetables

Prep time: 15 minutes | Cook time: 40 minutes | Serves 6

Olive oil cooking spray

2 large potatoes, cubed

2 carrots, sliced

1 small rutabaga, cubed

2 celery stalks, chopped

½ teaspoon smoked paprika

¼ cup plus 1 tablespoon olive oil, divided

2 rosemary sprigs

1 cup buckwheat groats

2 cups vegetable broth

2 garlic cloves, minced

½ yellow onion, chopped

1 teaspoon salt

1. Preheat the air fryer to 380ºF (193ºC). Lightly coat the inside of a 5-cup capacity casserole dish with

olive oil cooking spray. (The shape of the casserole dish will depend upon the size of the air fryer, but it needs to be able to hold at least 5 cups.)

2. In a large bowl, toss the potatoes, carrots, rutabaga, and celery with the paprika and ¼ cup olive oil.

3. Pour the vegetable mixture into the prepared casserole dish and top with the rosemary sprigs. Place the casserole dish into the air fryer and bake for 15 minutes.

4. While the vegetables are cooking, rinse and drain the buckwheat groats.

5. In a medium saucepan over medium-high heat, combine the groats, vegetable broth, garlic, onion, and salt with the remaining 1 tablespoon olive oil. Bring the mixture to a boil, then reduce the heat to low, cover, and cook for 10 to 12 minutes.

6. Remove the casserole dish from the air fryer. Remove the rosemary sprigs and discard. Pour the cooked buckwheat into the dish with the vegetables and stir to combine. Cover with aluminum foil and bake for an additional 15 minutes.

7. Stir before serving.

PER SERVING: Calories: 344; Total Fat: 13g; Saturated Fat: 2g; Protein: 8g; Total Carbohydrates: 50g; Fiber: 8g; Sugar: 4g; Cholesterol: 0mg

Farro Risotto with Fresh Sage

Prep time: 10 minutes | Cook time: 35 minutes | Serves 6

Olive oil cooking spray

1½ cups uncooked farro

2 ½ cups chicken broth

1 cup tomato sauce

1 yellow onion, diced

3 garlic cloves, minced

1 tablespoon fresh sage, chopped

½ teaspoon salt

2 tablespoons olive oil

1 cup Parmesan cheese, grated, divided

1. Preheat the air fryer to 380°F (193°C). Lightly coat the inside of a 5-cup capacity casserole dish with olive oil cooking spray. (The shape of the casserole dish will depend upon the size of the air fryer, but it needs to be able to hold at least 5 cups.)

2. In a large bowl, combine the farro, broth, tomato sauce, onion, garlic, sage, salt, olive oil, and ½ cup of the Parmesan.

3. Pour the farro mixture into the prepared casserole dish and cover with aluminum foil.

4. Bake for 20 minutes, then uncover and stir. Sprinkle the remaining ½ cup Parmesan over the top and bake for 15 minutes more.

5. Stir well before serving.

PER SERVING: Calories: 284; Total Fat: 10g; Saturated Fat: 3g; Protein: 12g; Total Carbohydrates: 40g; Fiber: 4g; Sugar: 3g; Cholesterol: 14mg